Before God

- A film by Britta Wauer
- Germany 2016
- 90 minutes
- available on DVD
  with English subtitles

www.rabbiwolff.com

Willy Wolff, now over 80 years old, has both a residence and a workplace in two different countries. As a State Rabbi he functions in the North-East of Germany and writes for the London "Times". He is a British citizen with German roots and delivers his sermons in Russian. In addition he loves yoga, Christmas carols and betting at horse races.

For more than three years, German filmmaker Britta Wauer and her team, have been following the State Rabbi of Mecklenburg-West Pomerania with the camera. In numerous conversations, Willy Wolff looks back over his eventful life, talks about his childhood in Berlin and Amsterdam, his career as a political correspondent in England and his lifelong desire to become a Rabbi.

Rabbi Wolff and the Essence of Life

Memories and Insights

Complied by
Britta Wauer

Original German version translated into English by
Bea Green

Translated into English by Bea Green

Bea Green was born in Munich in 1925 and was one of the 10,000 Jewish children who came to England on the Kindertransport, where she arrived, aged 14, in June 1939. She started school at Neyland House High School in Kent, and then in 1942 went to University College London where she graduated in 1946 with BA Hons. in Modern Languages. She then taught German and French at Clifton High School for Girls in Bristol and subsequently taught English in Lima, Peru at the Colegio Leon Pinelo. She returned to London in 1954 where she worked as a film sub-titler in French, Spanish and German.

Bea, who has three sons, married Dr Michael Green, an economist in1957, following which they spent two years in Colombo, Sri Lanka, returning to the UK in 1959 where she spent 29 years as a senior lecturer in English for foreign business students at City of London Polytechnic. From 1975 to 1995 she was a Magistrate at Richmond Court, London.

Bea is also the translator from German to English of "Journey into the Unknown" - the diary of holocaust survivor, Bertl Kaufmann

Original German version:
© 2016 Hentrich & Hentrich Verlag, Berlin
Dr. Nora Pester, Wilhelmstrasse 118
10963 Berlin, Germany
www.hentrichhentrich.de info@hentrichhentrich.de
English edition © James Leek 2016

First Edition German and English version: 2016

ISBN 978-1-78222-489-1

Production management of English edition by Into Print
• www.intoprint.net • +44 (0)1604 832149
Printed and bound in UK, USA and Australia by Lightning Source

Contents

Introduction

Words have always played a great part in my professional life, in the first place when I was a journalist for the English daily press then later and now as a Rabbi. But I have always refused to write anything autobiographical. There is a limit to the interest I have in myself. I much preferred the idea of writing about courageous women, eminent members of German Jewry and about post-war English politics.

I was taken aback when I saw myself described here as "probably the most unusual Rabbi in the world" as I considered myself more or less the same as dozens of other Rabbis of European congregations. True, not all of them had been journalists first, travelling through the world from Rome via Reykjavik with or without the British Foreign Secretary.

My family had escaped annihilation by emigrating very early. But it also had to pay a price for that. I come from an unhappy family and I never intended to share my story. It is stressful and difficult to do that. After my mother's death, I got rid of all the photo albums I could find. However, I did send just a few pictures to my nephew in America. I did not believe that anyone might be interested in them.

If there is anything in my life of which I am proud it is that I cared for and looked after both my grandmother as well as my mother at home right up to their death.

All this contributed to my own deep understanding of the variety of human destinies. Whether it also granted me wisdom I rather doubt. It is for others to make this judgment.

I hope reading this will interest you and give you pleasure.

Berlin, 1 March 2016

Rabbi William Wolff

The twin brothers Wilhelm (left) and Joachim sitting on the lap
of their nanny, on the right sister Ruth, Berlin summer 1927

Wolff Wolff

When my mother was pregnant her sister-in-law decided what name I should be given. That seriously annoyed my mother who thought that she too ought to have a say in this. However, my father's sister insisted that the oldest son should have the same name as the grandfather. She had been asking all along: "So how long is it before our little Wilhelm is born?"

My mother managed to counter this kind of domineering in two ways. On 13th February, an hour and a half after "Wilhelm" was born, she gave birth to a second boy, my twin brother, whom she called Joachim. She blessed me, however, with innumerable pet names. Never once in all her life did she call me "Wilhelm".

She did not know her husband's father who had died before my parents met each other. Originally grandfather's name was Wolff Wolff but that was one Wolff too many for him so he changed one to "Wilhelm". I am grateful to him for that, saving me from the fate of a double Wolff.

Wilhelm Wolff was a trained tailor and, at the turn of the century, he was in charge of the menswear department in a large store in Hannover. He looks very congenial on the photograph that I have of him. I ask myself sometimes what could have happened that his son, my father, turned out to be such a difficult person.

Alfred Wolff was already 44 when he married my mother. She was twenty years younger than he and her name was Charlotte, née Rothstein. Both came from German-Jewish families, but he was strictly orthodox. But this

Grandfather Wilhelm Wolff around 1900, Willy was named
after him

Willy Wolff, June 1928

was not obvious. German orthodox Jewish men did not generally have beards or sideburns and covered their heads only when they were praying or eating or occupied with religious writing. Being an orthodox Jew in those days meant observing the rules and regulations rather than wearing particular clothes. My father looked like every other man.

According to Jewish law, one is Jewish if one has a Jewish mother. Judaism is not concerned with the father's origin. If the father is a Jew but the mother is not, their children are considered as not Jewish. That was somewhat ironic in my case: I am a Jew because my mother was Jewish but she was not really interested in her Jewishness and was appalled when her oldest son confessed to wanting to become a Rabbi. But that was actually many years later when we had been living in London for decades and my first name had been anglicised to William.

We were living in the Hansa quarter of Berlin alongside the river Spree. My father used to go to the Synagogue of the orthodox Adass Yisrael community in Lessing Street. Today there is just a memorial with the names of the erstwhile famous members of the community. While I cannot remember Albert Einstein I well remember others, for example Ismael Elbogen who had written a seminal book about Jewish liturgy and also Rabbi Dr. Heinrich Cohn that everyone just called 'Heini'. I also recall Hermann Struck, the painter. On one occasion his brother Felix brought my sister Ruth home to us after my father had forgotten to bring her back from the Synagogue.

The house that we had lived in no longer exists. But I know that it was a large flat with many rooms. When, on a Saturday, after the Shabbat service, we were all eating lunch together and we had finished our soup, someone had to go to the door, open it and call down the corridor: "Next course!" So then our maid came from the kitchen, bringing the next course.

As was customary in bourgeois circles in those days, we had a nanny who looked after us three siblings. Once a week we had a woman that came to do our family laundry, both washing and ironing, quite inconceivable today. I did once read that the most important discovery of the 20th century was not the computer but the washing machine. I go along with that. Nothing in the 20th century has changed the life of women as much as the washing machine and the 'pill'.

Rubber factory

When my father was a young man he lived for a few years in London. From that time on he had good connections with England and represented several English firms in Germany. But he was also involved in a factory in Berlin-Weissensee, that is the "Standard Para Rubber Factory" that produced rubber mainly for medical purposes. Later, when we left Germany, his non-Jewish associate, Wilhelm Holzberg, became the sole managing director.

Interestingly enough, my father's business career ran parallel with the era of rubber. When rubber products were popular, his business flourished and when my father died, shortly after the Second World War, the use of rubber came to an end and was replaced by synthetic and plastic material.

Basically, my father was not particularly interested in us children. He was out and about on business all day and only came home around 7pm. Once my father took my twin brother and me to his office and the chaos on his desk was indescribable. My father was looking for a certain letter and pulled a sheet out from a big pile of papers. It was the paper he was looking for but I said to myself: "You'll never live like that!" But I have to confess, that is exactly how I live. I have inherited this untidiness from my father.

A fortnight after the Nazis came to power my twin and I had our 6th birthday. In April 1933, Joachim and I started at the Adass Yisrael school which was only a few minutes walk from our home.

We went to school in Berlin for only three months. It was then that my mother insisted that we should emigrate.

Mrs. Friedlander

When people asked my mother why we left Berlin as early as September 1933, she tells them the story of Mrs. Friedlander who lived in the Hansa quarter where we were living and where she worked as a seamstress. In those days there was a lot of mending of clothes, shortening, lengthening or taking in and both my mother and my grandmother were her customers.

Mrs. Friedlander had a daughter called Magda who

The siblings Ruth, Willy (centre) and Jo six months after their
arrival in Amsterdam, April 1934

had married a young politician whose first name was Joseph and his surname: Goebbels. That meant Mrs. Friedlander was the mother-in-law of the Reich Minister of Propaganda. So, when the Nazis came to power in 1933, my mother thought that because of our connection to Mrs. Friedlander, our names might possibly come soon to the attention of the Nazis, so she wanted to get away as soon as possible.

We got on to the night train the evening of 27th September 1933 and arrived in Amsterdam at 12.30 the next day.

Amsterdam

I was six years old when we came to Amsterdam. It became the city of my childhood and even today I like being there. We really liked being in Holland - all of us, except my father.

All we had when we arrived was our suitcases. My parents had nowhere to live. They had to find a flat, get their belongings from Berlin and start a new life. It must have been difficult to do that and look after three little children. So they decided to put them into a children's home. When I heard them talk about this I began to cry. I imagined I would never see my parents again. However, there was no discussion, we were sent to the children's home in Hilversum and, as far as I can remember, we were not unhappy.

Soon after our arrival, my father had a nervous breakdown. The situation he found himself in, in a country

Jo, Ruth and Willy (right) at Zandvoort in the Netherlands,
July 1935

that he did not know, where he had no function but had to support a young family, was too much for him. He was incapable of making any decision whatsoever.

My mother took him to Kreuzlingen in Switzerland, probably one of the best known and certainly the most expensive psychiatric clinic in Europe. He came back only nine months later when my mother had furnished a flat, brought the children to live with her and found them schools. She had coped with all this by herself and, in my opinion, shown organisational skills never before demanded from her.

There was no Jewish school in the part of Amsterdam we were living in. We went to a regular state school and never again to a Jewish school. I am very grateful for growing up in ordinary surroundings in contact with non-Jewish people.

My siblings and I learned quickly and spoke Dutch with each other. My twin brother and I were good pupils, but he was better than I. My sister went to a girls' high school where she had a maths teacher called Max Euwe. He was a chess grand master. You would think it was not necessary for him to teach maths. Today you can earn a small fortune with a title like that, but not in those days. All he got as world champion was honour and praise.

In Amsterdam we children were also lucky in that some of the male members of the large congregation in the Lekstraat that we belonged to decided to start a youth service. They did this very conscientiously by eliminating only very little from the liturgy which was different from what other communities did. The service of our childhood covered almost all the liturgy. Sometimes the young were even involved in it which made a deep impression on me. My brother was never particularly interested in religion while my sister and I were deeply involved so we liked going there.

Today, the Synagogue in the Lakstreet houses auctioneers. You can still see where the Torahs were kept and where the pulpit stood but the prayer hall now contains showcases with works of art behind glass. When I think back on that now, it pains me. I was, after all, present at the Synagogue's inauguration. But, unlike a church, a Synagogue is not a sacred place. You can do anything there - sing, dance, celebrate, even though it is officially a house of prayer.

Businessman

My father had a representative in Holland. The idea was that they would set up a business together. They did try but they did not succeed.

At the beginning my father did have an office in Amsterdam but, in order to save money, he worked from home which made my parents' relationship with each other more and more difficult. While one can never make such judgments, I do believe that my parents' marriage might perhaps have lasted longer in Berlin. There my father was out of the house on business all day, Saturday morning he was in the Synagogue, in the afternoon there were social occasions at home or with relatives and in the evening my parents went out with friends. All this came to an end in Amsterdam. They were on their own and dependant on each other.

Charlotte Wolff, née Rothstein, at Zandvoort in July 1935

There are people who say that it was very prudent of my parents to leave Holland and that they felt it likely that Hitler would get there too. That is very nice of them but I don't think that was the case. My father just could not cope with life in Holland, neither with business there nor with the language. Even when he was a young man - he was born in Hannover - he had already lived a few years in England and it was always in Germany that he represented English firms. Since things did not work out in Amsterdam he spent more and more time in England earning his living there. So it was only a question of time when he would get his family to join him.

My mother had created a new life for herself. She was in her late thirties and had two flourishing circles of friends, one of German Jewish emigrants and another of Dutch friends. She was far from delighted at the prospect of moving to England. She told my father that she would stay until the twins had completed primary school. But because she kept on postponing our departure, my father phoned at the end of August 1939 and insisted: "Come now, at once!"

So that is why we left Amsterdam very quickly without furniture, just with bare necessities. We travelled to the Hook of Holland and from there by ship to Harwich. We stepped on English soil the evening of the 28th of August. Three days later Hitler marched into Poland and on 3rd September England and France declared war on Germany.

London

My father had already bought a house in north west London in early 1939. Hendon is today a very Jewish district and even then my father moved there as the Synagogue was within walking distance.

The United Synagogue in Hendon was very modern, the building was four years old and they had a wonderful Cantor, David Koussevitzky who came from Lithuania. He had a beautiful, strong voice and knew how to stage-manage himself. When he went round the Synagogue with the Torah scroll, he was aware of his gait, walking with great dignity and fascinating personality. It was a real experience to listen to him but at the same time he overshadowed many other Rabbis. Their sermons had to be especially good to compete with him. Koussevitzky made a lifelong impression on me. It was he who showed me how important music and dignity were at a religious service.

Unfortunately, after the war, Koussevitzky received a considerably higher offer from New York. The London Synagogue community had not allowed him to give concerts while the Americans had no problem with him doing that. So he moved to New York which was a great loss to us but the right decision for him. He became world famous in New York. Later he also appeared in London a few times where he performed not only Jewish liturgical music but also Italian arias. When we saw each other again on one of these occasions he told me that, had he remained in England, he would have arranged for me to be trained as a Cantor. But, as things turned out, there was no one else to do that.

The siblings Jo, Ruth and Willy (right) on the occasion of the
twin's Bar Mitzvah, London in spring 1940

War

Looking back now, the remainder of my childhood was actually very lonely. There were no relatives around - they had either stayed behind or emigrated to other countries - and one had to establish new friendships. And that was not always easy.

Our parents' marriage finally collapsed. It was no pleasure to be there and to observe it. The separation also destroyed our social life. As a result, several families, especially those who were orthodox, avoided us.

The outbreak of war led to an initial closure of schools. So it was not until January 1940, shortly before our 13th birthday, that my twin brother and I were enrolled in a school again. The first thing that our history teacher said was: "You are three months behind and you have to catch up yourselves with what I would have been teaching." My brother and I were the only ones who took the trouble to go through the material in the history book from cover to cover. To understand everything we had to constantly resort to the dictionary. As a result, once we had read the whole history book, we had learned not only history but, fairly quickly, the English language.

Along with our 13th birthday and our Bar Mitzvah, we became fully-fledged members of the Jewish community. Just two weeks earlier another set of twins, the brothers Kennard, had celebrated their Bar Mitzvah in our synagogue. As it was so unusual for two sets of twins to celebrate this event so close to each other, it was reported in the weekly paper the "Jewish

Chronicle". That was the first time my name appeared in a newspaper.

In England we also attended the religious services for children and young people, but I found they lacked gravity. They were simplified to the point where we could not identify, completely different from what we had become used to in Holland.

Instead, my brother and I were receiving religious instruction from the former Berlin Rabbi Dr. Moritz Freier. I am always rather sad that he is almost forgotten today, whereas his wife, Mrs. Recha Freier, became a celebrity in German Jewish history. She was the founder in 1933 of "Youth Aliyah", an organisation that, by enabling thousands of young people to leave Germany, helped to save their lives.

Moritz Freier had been a very good preacher in Berlin where he looked after three Synagogues: in the Rykestrasse, Heidereutergasse and Kaiserstrasse. In London he was living on his own in near poverty. He was earning his living by giving lessons and that is how he came to us.

We were living just one and a half kilometres from an RAF airbase and when, in September 1940 the bomb attacks on London started, that clearly became a worthwhile target. Bombs dropped every evening but one got used to it. The first few days I went into the air raid shelter but I could not sleep there. It was too cramped and too hot. So I just stayed at home.

In 1944 the pilotless, insidious, V bombs hit London. One could hear them approach but the next moment

Photo of Willy (left) his father Alfred Wolff and brother Jo
around 1943 in London

the engine stopped. We knew they were about to drop but where? On your doorstep or a couple of miles away? A couple of miles away one of the V bomb came down and killed the owners of the house. But nothing happened to us. We were spared.

I am not a military historian but I think the lesson we can draw from the Second World War is that wars cannot be won by airplanes. They rather strengthen people's will to resist. You need ground forces that capture towns and countries. The Nazis destroyed Rotterdam and Coventry and the British finished by destroying Dresden. But that did not shorten the war. Basically, it hardly affected the course of the war. That is my view but historians may or may not confirm it.

The way into journalism

When I was 16 years old I was asked at school what profession I wished to pursue. I told them that I should like to become either a journalist or a Rabbi. I wanted to become a Rabbi when I was four or five years old and still in Berlin. And journalism just interested me.

Miss Davis, the senior French teacher, had been told by the Head Teacher to give the pupils career's advice. She had no idea how one became either a Rabbi or a journalist but she thought: "Wolff is good in French!" and got me a small grant to attend the French school in London. So, in 1943 at the Lycée Francais I not only learned to speak fluent French but obtained qualifications in bilingual office work which included short-hand and typing. I can still look into mid-air and type with nine fingers. Most entries in my diary are in short-hand, not because I want to be secretive but because it is quicker. To this day I am grateful to Miss Davis for the education I got at the French school.

I had to learn pretty quickly to earn money. Further education was out of the question so I applied for a job at Reuters, the international news agency. At that time I still observed orthodox rules and asked at the interview if I could have Saturday off to attend the service at the Synagogue. In return I could work at Christmas, Easter and other Christian holy days. Jimmy Green, the principal, just said: "We work seven days a week here and I don't think I can make an exception because that would be unfair to the others." I did understand that and got a small office job at a Zionist organisation. But then, only three or four weeks later, Green contacted me and said he had talked to his colleagues. Nobody objected to me having Saturday off. So that is when I started working at Reuters.

It was the last year of the war and I was in High Barnet on the outskirts of London where Reuters had its radio receiving station. The press agency used a system named after its inventor, Mr. Hell. In English it was called "ticker machine". It issued strips of paper with the news on it, not with Morse dots but with letters. I listened to the broadcasts from central Europe and wrote them down, for example, the daily report from the German military high command. It was regarded as of military importance and it was my first paid job.

Orthodoxy

Judaism, like all religions, is multifaceted. There is the choice between the ultra orthodox, the orthodox and liberal Judaism as well as the conservatives and others. Religious life everywhere tends to splinter resulting in different trends. I am no expert but Islam has Shiites and Sunnis and in Christendom there is the Roman Catholic and the Protestant Church, the Greek Orthodox and the Anglican Church and others. There are different groups and anyone can find the setting in which he or she feels comfortable.

On reaching the age of 20 I left orthodoxy behind or it left me. There were two reasons for that. For one, orthodoxy is very fundamentalist. Orthodox opinion, for example, maintains that God himself dictated every word in the five books of Moses. But when one reads the text that is really not possible. There are a number of contradictions, which would mean that when God dictated the fourth book to Moses, He had forgotten what He had said in the first or second book. So that made no sense to me. That was the theological reason for me to say good-bye to orthodoxy.

But there was a sociological reason too. Once my parents' marriage collapsed, my mother lived with another man for a number of years although she was still married to my father. That was not acceptable to the orthodox. It was only after my father had died that she could marry my stepfather. So there were certain difficulties that made strictly orthodox life unbearable for me.

My sister chose a different route. She left what had been German orthodoxy and became ultra orthodox. She withdrew, as it were, into ultra orthodoxy and had basically very little contact with the world around her. The ultra orthodox do live a life away from the rest of the world. The Christian concept would regard it as rather similar to living in a convent but Judaism does not have convents where same-sex people live together. Judaism regards family life as very important.

My sister married an ultra-orthodox man and moved to Gateshead in the north of England and had six children, three sons and three daughters. They, too, had a number of offspring but I do not know most of them. It is just that they, too, are ultra orthodox which means they live a somewhat secluded life, making it irrelevant whether it is in Israel or America.

I do get on well with two or three of my nephews. One of them lives in New York, the other one in Cincinnati and Jerusalem. I am also in close touch with a granddaughter. They care about me and frequently phone me. Although I am a Liberal Rabbi which basically would not be recognised by them, we accept each other as we are. I do not have serious theological discussions with them and, anyway, they do not want to hear my sermons!

Undated portrait of Willy Wolff, London in the 1950's

Father

My father died in November 1946 in the psychiatric clinic in Shenley in Hertfordshire. Earlier, the clinic had informed us that he was not well, but when my Mother and I got to Shenley, he was already dead. He had been refusing to eat and it was planned to force-feed him. The tube went down the respiratory tract, which caused him to suffocate.

My father did not make it easy for people to like him. He was domineering and he laid down the law. But there must have been a time when he was charming otherwise my Mother would not have fallen in love with him. Because it had been in no way an arranged marriage.

Many years later, some 30 years after my father's death, when I was driving to Poland with my mother, I took a wrong turn that took us through Wroclaw, that used to be Breslau. That had not been our plan. Suddenly my mother turned to me and, looking out of the window, said: "Could you stop a second?" She wanted me to drive three houses further back and said: "That's where my first fiancé lived!"

The man that she had planned to marry was called Georg Schragenheim and was my father's cousin. When she attended a family celebration with him she got to know his cousin, Alfred Wolff. The rest is history. The engagement was dissolved and the next one established. That is why I am here.

It was always difficult for me to understand what my parents saw in each other. In my view they did not suit each other at all. There was this great age difference

The only remaining photo where my parents are seen together:
Charlotte and Alfred Wolff, probably in Amsterdam around
1935

between them and absolutely no shared interests. My father came from Hannover and was very orthodox while my Berlin mother could not care less about religion.

With the end of her marriage to my father, my mother wanted nothing more to do with Judaism. My sister becoming ultra-orthodox made things difficult for my mother as there was so much to consider- different crockery for different food, different holy days and different behaviour. When, later on, I wanted to become a Rabbi, she was afraid that it would happen to her a second time but with her oldest son.

Health

Because I wanted to continue with my studies after my father's death, I attended the London School of Economics focusing on International Relations and Economics. But during my first year I became very ill. I was incapable of work, stayed mostly in bed and no one knew what to do with me. It was only three years later that a friend of my mother's recommended a homeopath in Geneva. His name was Pierre Schmidt and he eventually concluded that my liver and my kidneys did not function properly. So, first of all, I was not to eat any meat or sausages, which did me a lot of good. The moment I stopped eating meat, my kidney problems vanished. That was a kind of liberation. I have not touched meat ever since, but I do eat fish.

As I am also seriously allergic to milk products I became interested in naturopathy which has been important to me all my life.

It was in the 1960's, when I discovered yoga and now spend some fifteen minutes every day sitting in the lotus position - the real one! Some yoga teachers just sit with crossed legs but the real lotus position requires the right foot to rest on the left thigh and the left foot on the right thigh. I find it beneficial and relaxing and I believe it keeps my joints mobile.

If I get home late in the evening, still feeling very animated, I sit in the lotus position which calms me. And then I fall asleep right away.

Fun driving

The first car I owned was a small 1932 Austin. It was an old banger but it was mine and I was very proud of it. The brakes no longer worked properly. On one occasion when I was about to park in front of my mother's house, the brakes failed and I had to reverse so as to use the curb to stop the car from rolling down the hill. But for me everything seemed all right.

At that time I was working as a reporter in the town of Slough, near Windsor, 20 miles west of London. It was my first job for a newspaper. There were no schools for journalism at that time and one started in that profession by joining a local paper and learning the trade from scratch. If one proved oneself adept one could climb the ladder and, at some point, wind up working for one of the London daily papers.

At that time, Slough was used as a 'guinea pig' to test traffic security measures. It was an accepted experiment

William Wolff with his Honda, Henley-on-Thames, 2015

and every Tuesday or Wednesday morning at 11am there was a meeting at the Town Hall with the Chief of Police and other transport officers. I was sent there to write a report for the "Slough Observer". Just when I got to the Town Hall the Chief of Police stopped behind me and as we were walking in together, he said: "Well, Wolff, the first thing we have to do to make Slough a safer place is to get rid of your car." I took the hint, got rid of the Austin and bought a new car, a somewhat newer car.

I cannot imagine life without driving. In the little village where I live, I depend on it. Some ten years ago my driving licence was withdrawn for six months as I had accumulated too many endorsements. It was difficult but I did not cheat. I did not touch the car for six months. There was no longer a bus service in my village and I had to walk for half an hour to the next village every morning. From there I took a bus shortly after 7 o'clock to the next town and from there I could take a train. I still remember: my driving ban expired on 29 October, which happened to be the birthday of my sister Ruth. Come midnight I drove around briefly just to celebrate that I could drive again. And I told myself: I must never let that happen again.

My brother

My twin brother and I were not identical. I don't know if we looked like each other. Some people thought we did, the same number of people thought we did not. The best answer I ever got to that question was: "If I'd seen your brother in the street without knowing who he was, I would have wondered who he reminded me of."

He, unlike me who had no gift for mathematics, was good at languages and science. There was even competition among the teachers. Some wanted him to study science while others wanted him to continue with Latin. In the end he was allowed to attend both courses, which was quite exceptional.

After school he went on to study chemistry but after a year he decided to become a specialist in German studies. He became a student at the University of Birmingham where he obtained an Honours degree. That meant he could obtain an academic appointment.

Job offers appeared in The Times and as I, a journalist, read the papers, I kept a look-out for a job for him. The first one I found was in Southampton, in the south of England. But when my brother went for an interview, the position had already been filled. The next advertisement for a post as a specialist in German studies was in Perth, at the University of Western Australia. Jo sent his application and all the details and received an offer of the job as lecturer by return of post. There were no further questions, no conversations. It was an offer of a permanent job that my brother accepted. That is how it was in those days.

The academic year in Australia starts in March. As flights from Europe to Australia were unaffordable, my brother went on a ship in February 1956 to his destination half a world away. It took six weeks. Because of the Suez Canal conflict, their route took them round the southern tip of Africa.

Macmillan

The Egyptian president, Abdel Gamar Nassar, declared the Suez Canal to be Egyptian property in 1956 and prohibited transit. Britain and France with Israeli support tried to retake it but without success. It was the first time that the erstwhile sphere of influence exercised by the British and the French, had become ineffective. It was a deep humiliation for both former colonial powers and proved that both states were no longer world powers.

The Suez Canal crisis was one of the most impressive experiences for me as a young journalist. The then Prime Minister, Anthony Eden, did try to assert himself in this conflict, but without success. I remember that it was Robert Boothby - at that time just a backbencher - who defined the crucial debates in the House of Commons. Boothby was seriously charismatic and capable of leading subtle arguments. When Anthony Eden lost and Harold Macmillan became Prime Minister, it was on the cards that Boothby would be offered a ministerial post. Instead, Macmillan raised him to the ranks of aristocracy and he became Baron Boothby. That was a beautiful gesture but it also meant the end of his political career. A peer becomes automatically a member of the House of Lords and, once in the House of Lords, loses political influence.

I found it incredible not only that Macmillan elevated

his party colleague to the aristocracy but also that Boothby accepted it. Boothby could have refused. He had his political supporters in Aberdeen in Scotland and they would have re-elected him.

It was only later that I understood the background. Harold Macmillan was a great personality, even more significant then than it is acknowledged today. He came from a well-to-do Scottish family and was married to one of the daughters of the Duke of Devonshire, Lady Dorothy. But not long after their wedding, his wife had started an affair with another Conservative, the politician Robert Boothby. The affair lasted many years and one of the children in this marriage was said not to be Macmillan's but Boothby's. Macmillan had to cope with that so, when he became Prime Minister in January 1957, this was his solution. It must have given Macmillan great satisfaction to make this cuckold politically impotent by officially ennobling him.

Little Paddock

Although I had imagined myself living in a city, I fancied a home in the country. I was considering the south of Buckinghamshire or the small town of Marlow on the Thames. But when I started looking round, I realised that I could not afford that area. So I started looking round further west and found the small town of Henley. I went to the estate agent who mentioned among other properties, four bungalows that were being planned in a village.

I had never heard of that village and thought: "Well,

let's have a look and see what's going on." I drove there and was rather surprised that they thought they could manage to build four bungalows on this small plot. The way I saw it, there was only space for one. But then I said to myself, if I could have the end house, with a view across fields and meadows, I'd like that.

It sounds ridiculous today but I went back to the estate agent, put £25 on the table and reserved that house for myself. Of course, that was worth a lot more then. A year later I moved in.

There was a small garden in front of the house and a big one at the back but, because I'm not keen on gardening, I immediately decided: it will be just grass. That turned out to be very practical as I had friends visiting me and we were all much younger, they brought their small children who could run happily around on the grass. It all worked beautifully.

The postal service insisted that my house should have a name and I could make suggestions. This, however, took rather a long time because in this or that village there already was a house with the same name. Finally, they allowed me to use the name "Little Paddock".

My sister Ruth, who was the older sibling, always wanted to know what was going on in the life of her younger brothers. So she wanted to see my new home. She was only mildly enthusiastic. She could not understand why I wanted to live in the countryside.

Sister Ruth with her daughter Rahel and Willy in England, end of the 1950's

My sister

I am still moved when I think of the last conversation I had with my sister. It was shortly before Christmas 1964 when she had come to London with her husband and friends for a wedding celebration. Before going back up north she wanted to pop in to see my mother. I had been out that evening returning to my parental home just after midnight when my sister got into her car to drive back.

Ruth and I had agreed earlier that I would visit her in a few weeks time, which is what I did regularly once or twice a year. As the train would arrive in Newcastle only around 11pm, Ruth said, like a typical older sister: "I'll wait up for you but if I get too tired, I'll go to bed. I won't lock the door and you know which room you're sleeping in and I'll put a hot water bottle in your bed."

Probably anyone who has grown up with siblings knows how caring an older sister can be. But when this sister is 40 years old and she tells her 38-year-old brother that she would put a hot water bottle in his bed it shows clearly how very good this relationship must have been.

That was the last thing my sister said to me. Two hours later she lay dead on the road. There were six people in the car. Nothing happened to five of them but Ruth was dead.

My brother-in-law phoned at eight o'clock next morning and asked to speak to me. My mother asked at once: "What happened to little Ruth?" and I had to tell her. That was awful.

There was an inquest a few months later but no one who had been in that car said who had been driving it. They all lied because the driver did not have a valid driving licence. I found that out only much later. At that time it was important for me to know that her children would stay in touch with their grandmother.

David Owen

I had always had great respect for politicians but I was not always greatly impressed by them. In a sense, we were on the same playing field. The politicians realised that they needed the press and we journalists relied on information. It was a mutual relationship.

The Daily Mirror that I worked for as a journalist had bought a Sunday paper published in southwest England in the 1960's. One of our journalists was sent to Plymouth to become the editor. The paper had been seriously neglected and did not have a political correspondent. So, a colleague of mine who was now running that paper asked me to write a piece about politics every Sunday but with a special interest for the Southwest. I did not know much about the area but, as it was shortly after the election in spring 1966 with many new MP's in the House of Commons, I thought: "Perhaps I could interview some of the new MP's. I'll see who represents the Southwest and get some material for the next few weeks!"

So that is how I started interviewing the new MP's. One of whom was a young doctor from Plymouth, a psychiatrist called David Owen. We got on well as there was, fortunately good human chemistry between us. He was a very intelligent person, and highly interested in the world around him. That is why he had become a politician. He was competent and soon became a government Minister.

We often had lunch together and one day he asked me: "Can you give me some advice? A friend from New

Willy Wolff as a journalist in London, around 1972

York is coming to visit me. Where can I take her? To the theatre? What is worth showing her?" I told him what in my opinion was worth seeing and I think my suggestions were not bad. A few months later they were engaged to each other and, in due course, got married. The first or second weekend after their wedding they came to have a meal with me, and it was not long before he became a Minister. But that is how our friendship had started.

Towards the end of the 70's David Owen became Foreign Secretary but later he left the Labour Party and together with others started a new Social Democratic Party. But even when he was leader of the Left I could call him at home to ask him questions. That was of great value to me.

As a former member of the Cabinet, David Owen was almost automatically made a Peer of the Realm. That is customary in England. His name now is "Baron Owen of the City of Plymouth". But when I talk to him I still call him David and he calls me Willy.

Germany

It was 35 years before I set foot on German soil again. It happened unexpectedly when I was accompanying Michael Stewart, the Foreign Secretary, on a trip. He was very competent but without any charisma and is no longer remembered. I meanwhile, was responsible for Foreign Affairs at the Daily Mirror and accompanied Stewart in 1968 for talks in Moscow. On our return to London he surprisingly arranged a halfway stop in Bonn to meet Willy Brandt. At that time Brandt was not

Willy Wolff (left) during a BBC German language broadcast at
the Goethe Institute London, January 1973

yet Chancellor but rather Foreign Secretary who had been expected in London. For some reason, this visit had never taken place.

So the British Foreign Secretary landed in Cologne and, since I was a member of the British delegation and in the same plane, it was my first visit to Germany since our emigration in 1933. It was a moving moment for me but there was also an ironic touch to it: I spent this short stay in Germany on English soil since we correspondents waited at the British Embassy while Michael Stewart met Willy Brandt. Officially the British Embassy is British territory.

I saw quite a lot of Willy Brandt. As Foreign Secretary he visited London frequently and we journalists who were responsible for reporting on foreign affairs were always invited when he came here. I was also a co-founder of an association of journalists that, once a month, organised a lunch at one of the big London hotels, the Dorchester. We always invited a guest who would give a talk after the meal and would answer our questions. The German Embassy was eager to have Willy Brandt attend one of our lunches when he was in London. This became an exciting event and a challenge, organising the seating arrangements for our distinguished and perhaps sensitive guests.

I am only a moderate admirer of Willy Brandt. He did seriously achieve something with his *Ostpolitik* and, without doubt, he is one of the most significant figures in German post-war history. But I cannot say that I found him likeable. There was no personal connection between him and me. Willy Brandt was not interested in men but rather in any woman that was around. He pursued every woman to a degree that was not appropriate for a prominent German Minister.

Good old Harold

The paper I worked for, The Daily Mirror had, at that time, a circulation of more than five million. It is much less today. The editor was a journalistic genius and the paper was seriously influential.

As political correspondent I was assigned to the Prime Minister and travelled with him everywhere in England but also abroad. One Friday evening, during the 1970 election, Harold Wilson, the then Prime Minister, a very pleasant and competent person, was visiting small towns north of London. I thought it might be worthwhile following him so as to write a report for the Sunday paper, the Sunday Mirror. So I went with him that Friday evening.

Wilson went from one town hall to the next, speaking at each one, of course always the same speech. He was totally without escort, unthinkable today. He had no driver nor police protection, no one from his office, no one. It was just he and I. We knew each other well and got on well with each other.

Whenever we came out of a building, his followers were standing there, patted him on the back, calling out: "Good old Harold! Good old Harold!" They literally patted him very hard, but with the best intentions rather overdid it. Our cars were some 100 to 150 yards away.

SUNDAY MIRROR edition of 7 June 1970 with William
Wolff's leader about Prime Minister Harold Wilson's election
campaign

Wilson turned to me and said: "Willy, we'd better run!" and so we ran. There was just nobody to protect this man, the Prime Minister, and it went on all evening.

I got home late and was so incensed that I sat down and wrote a report to the Editor in Chief: "This cannot go on. Something has to be done." When I got to the office next day, nobody mentioned anything about it. Nobody said: "Thank you for informing us about this. We'll get another journalist to do this and that…." not a word.

That evening, as I usually did, I took the first edition of the Sunday paper home, sat down and skimmed through the pages: pages 3, 4, 5, 6 - no report from me. Nothing. Oh well, I thought, you've done your duty. Let's have a quick look on the front page. What are the headlines? What will sell the paper today?

The only subject covered on the front page was: the Prime Minister without security guards was mobbed. That was the Sunday edition. Monday morning, between eleven and half past eleven, the Prime Minster's private office phoned and thanked me, saying: "At nine o'clock this morning Scotland Yard came to Downing Street to discuss what protection could be provided for the Prime Minister."

That was the power of the press. With as big a circulation as this paper's - and it was the biggest in England, it was also of political significance. I derived great pleasure working there. There were always exciting moments.

Then a new Editor in Chief was appointed, Michael Christiansen, who wanted rather more scandal. He realised pretty quickly that I was not the right person for that and I knew it, too. He demoted me and gave me the name of "European Editor", which did not mean much at that time. The European Union was not yet significant and the UK had only recently become a member. Looking back now, I think I could have done something in that position. But at that time I did not find it interesting.

So, after twelve years at the Daily Mirror I left. They were very generous and continued paying me my salary for another year. I became a freelance journalist and wrote for the London evening paper, the "Evening News".

Lord Rothermere

One of the great diplomats in the post-war period was the German Karl-Günther von Hase. He was ambassador in London for seven years, which is an exceptionally long period. Normally, diplomats stay no longer than four or five years. He was extremely popular and very valuable at this time when the UK wanted to join the European Union while there was also much resistance. It would have been appropriate to entrust him with a post at Washington or Paris but both situations were already occupied. So they offered him to be Ambassador for NATO in Brussels but he refused. In the end he became the General Administrator of German Television, ZDF, and stayed there till his retirement.

In 1977, when he left London, I wrote an editorial about him for the Evening News in which I described the great impression that he had made in London. When the article appeared, the Editor-in-Chief told me: "Lord Rothermere wants to talk to you." Rothermere was the owner of the paper. I thought: "That'll be interesting" and made an appointment. When I went to see Rothermere, he said sternly: "Sit down, Mr. Wolff. Please explain how you came to write this article about the Ambassador. How could you claim that anyone in London of consequence would have been a guest of his? I was never invited there!"

That went on for about ten minutes when the approach changed completely and he showed great interest in what was going on in politics and wanted to know how this or that could be interpreted. I remember telling him that Minister of State, David Owen, would go far and, in fact, two years later he became Foreign Secretary. We had a lively conversation when his secretary came in and said: "My Lord, so-and-so has been waiting to see you for twenty minutes," so Lord Rothermere said, apologetically, that I should get in touch with him again if there was something interesting to report.

It was only later that I discovered that his wife, Lady Rothermere, an actress, who played a significant role in London society, was a friend of the American Ambassador, Anne Armstrong. Lady Rothermere was indignant that her friend, whose term of office came to an end at the same time, had not been mentioned in the newspaper article while the German Ambassador, by whom she had never been invited, had been mentioned. So Lord Rothermere chided me at his wife's request, and having done his duty, we had a pleasant conversation.

The vegetarian restaurant "The Whole Meal" in 297 Upper
Street, London, Islington in 1971 - a delighted customer
painted the shop window

The Whole Meal

Time was when I really enjoyed cooking and often invited from eight to twelve people for lunch on a Sunday. Today my former dining room is full of books and I cannot now imagine how I could have catered for so many people.

One day, Patricia, a colleague from the advertising department with whom I often had lunch, told me that she considered starting a vegetarian restaurant. My immediate reaction was: "I'll be in on it" but then promptly forgot about it. Months later, it must have been beginning of 1971, Patricia came to me and said: "I've found it." I had no idea what she was talking about but she was referring to the premises for the restaurant. I didn't have the courage to say that I'd better think about it some more.

The rooms were in Upper Street, Islington, North London. This part of London had deteriorated for decades but was becoming trendy. We called the restaurant "The Whole Meal" which had a double meaning: one of them means wholemeal food, it was after all a vegetarian restaurant, and the other meaning implied a "Complete Meal".

The restaurant was open every day and a great success from the start. There was a queue on Sundays. Then the local magazine "TIME OUT" published an enthusiastic review, describing "The Whole Meal" as one of the best vegetarian restaurants in town. We could only just cope with the resulting demand. I did do the cooking there at weekends but during the week I worked at the paper.

After a few months I said to myself: "You cannot cope with that. Do you want to be a journalist or a restaurant owner?"

It was absolutely clear to me that I wanted to remain in journalism. So I left the restaurant to Patricia. She was not good as a manager and within months debts mounted. We had to close shop and I paid the debts. That was the end of the restaurant, not a glorious bit of history.

But Patricia and I have remained friends to this day and her daughter, who had not been born at that time, is now my goddaughter.

Family

If there is anything in my in my life that I regret then it is the fact that I never married and never created a family. I can hardly believe that I am as old as I am but have no children or grandchildren.

One of the first commandments in the Bible is: "Be fruitful and multiply!" Reading it one could interpret it as a blessing or God's wish but Judaism regards it as a commandment. That is why Rabbis are supposed to marry to fulfil this commandment. If they are orthodox they mostly have many children. I have to confess: this is a great absence in my life.

It is difficult to explain. It may have something to do with the fact that my own family had been a very unhappy one. I could not imagine that a marriage - and in those days one had marriages rather than relationship - would allow one to lead a happy life.

But perhaps there are more mundane reasons. As I was, for three years, very ill in my mid-twenties, significant years passed during which most people of that age would have found their life partners. During that period of time I disappeared from everyday life.

Then there was my work for daily newspapers, which meant that I was working evenings, sometimes till midnight and even one o'clock in the morning. I did not mind that but it meant that I could not go to evening events or to parties because I was working. And it was work that I enjoyed and that I found interesting. But the drawback was a lack of social life. Looking back it was actually more important than I thought it was at the time. There were one or two occasions when things went wrong and I remained on my own.

But I am not the sort of person who would be depressed by this. I try to enjoy life and get as much fun as possible. If anything in life was no longer fun I made sure to change to something that gave me pleasure.

Willy Wolff in the corridor of his house "Little Paddock"
in 2015

The wish to become a Rabbi

While I had little contact with religious Judaism for many years, I was always conscious of my Jewishness. And the desire to become a Rabbi recurred again and again. One morning I woke up, I was already more than fifty years old, and I said to myself: "It's now or never!" I was quite certain that I wanted to train to be a Rabbi. I had, meanwhile, learned about liberal Judaism that I had not come across before and it appealed to me. So I thought: "Perhaps it's not too late to make a contribution there."

At that time, the head of the Liberal Movement in England, asked me to work on his monthly magazine which had been rather boring. So I took the opportunity and asked him on one occasion whether it would be possible for me to attend the liberal rabbinical seminary in London. By chance, the Board that decided on admissions, had a meeting two days later. He took me along to this meeting, and, much to my surprise, I was accepted for this course of study. The Rabbinical Seminary was to start in October 1979 at the Leo Baeck College.

My mother was appalled that I wanted to become a Rabbi. She was the last person I told. She was in a German spa, as she was every summer. I had said to myself: "Everyone knows that you are going to a rabbinical seminary in autumn except your mother. Perhaps the time has come to tell her." So I wrote her a letter. When we saw each other next she just said: "That was a surprise." And that's how it was left. She was not delighted.

On her birthday, a few months later, twelve guests were sitting round the table. I remember clearly when, at lunch, a good friend of my mother's asked her: "Weren't you pleased that Willy decided to become a Rabbi?" And my mother who, at the age of about 70, had started saying openly what was in her mind without considering possible consequences, replied: "No, not at all. I'd have preferred him to remain a journalist." Then there was a shocked silence in the room, no one moved, no one said anything and I thought: "You've got to think of something else to talk about."

The Rabbinical Seminary

I was not altogether unprepared for the seminar. I did have a certain basic knowledge as I had come from an orthodox background. The other students were twenty or thirty years younger than I but that did not bother me. In my opinion it is not true that learning becomes more difficult with age, to some extent it becomes easier. I was better at dealing with grammar having learned other languages before. It was not more difficult but one had to work at it and that took time.

In the first year we learned the grammar of biblical Hebrew and after that year I realised that I was not good at it. In my third year I thought: "You really have to learn this." And I realised that I needed more discipline and enrolled at the University of London for the Hebrew exam, which I passed with good results but as I still thought that my Hebrew was not good enough, I enrolled for the advanced course. Then I suddenly realised: I won't be able to cope with this on my own. So I had private lessons with a lecturer. But every time he gave me back my homework much of it was crossed out with red ink. So I said to him: "If this goes on, Dr. Weitzmann, I won't pass the exam." And he answered: "You are absolutely right. You won't pass the exam."

That is when I started to go through all the grammar again from beginning to end. And that worked after a lot of effort. However, the weekend before the exam I was so agitated I could not sleep, but then I told myself: "You are not 18 any more. Just don't worry!"

The exam was difficult but I managed it. I knew how to deal with the Hebrew texts and can still deal with them today. That facilitates the preparation for the Synagogue service.

In orthodox Synagogues the biblical text is melodically recited, possibly similar to the Gregorian chant in churches. Many Liberal Synagogues do not do this but it is very important for me to preserve this tradition also in Liberal Judaism. Firstly, because it is an essential part of me, as it was how I experienced it from childhood and secondly I thought it wrong to lose a tradition like this.

Every sentence in the Torah has its specific melody that one has to know. There is no fixed model that one has to learn. One has to work on it, sentence by sentence. In the course of my rabbinic studies, I was sent to a small community to lead the service. I realised that to perform the text properly I needed to find a music teacher. I don't remember how I found him but he was a retired opera singer who called himself Finelli. When

I sang something for him he said soberly: "Your voice is not impressive but we can try to develop it." So I took singing lessons with him for a few years. One day he said to me: "You know, Mr. Wolff, what I appreciate in you? You are completely consistent. You make the same mistakes again and again."

Thatcher

It was during Margaret Thatcher's period in office that I was pursuing my studies. She became Prime Minister only a few months before I started my rabbinic studies in May 1979. I was 52 when I began my studies and I told myself: "You can only study if you have the same income as before." That is why I continued working as a journalist and wrote a political column for the Scottish Sunday paper the "Sunday Mail". I would go to the House of Commons on Thursday evenings to get a feeling of the debates and on Friday afternoon to Downing Street where we correspondents of the Sunday papers would get background information from the Prime Minister's spokesperson.

In my opinion, Mrs. Thatcher was not as splendid as her supporters claimed nor did she deserve to be disdained by so many. My personal memory of her is that she always felt under attack and that put her immediately on the defensive.

One Friday afternoon, it must have been 1984, we Sunday paper correspondents came as usual to Downing Street. That day the Speaker said: "We'll go up to see the Prime Minister today." So that is how we were sitting in a small circle with Mrs. Thatcher. At that time the miners had been on strike for several months and it was a reminder of the strike ten years earlier, when coal reserves had been exhausted, electricity was rationed and offices and factories worked only a three-day week. That is what brought Edward Heath's leadership to an end. When, years later, Margaret Thatcher was Prime Minister, she was determined that that would not happen during her term of office. She had a massive reserve of coal, ready for any possible strike. So when, in March 1984, the miners, as was expected, started another strike because of closures or privatisation of the mines, she did not arrange meetings with the unions or do anything else.

As we were a small group and therefore in a position to ask Thatcher whatever we wanted, I asked her what, in her opinion, was the reason the miners were able to continue to strike for months and survive. Even before I had come to the end of my question, she pointed a finger at me and gave me a lecture. Government, she said, can neither be blackmailed nor make admissions. Well, that had not been implied in my question but that was Mrs. Thatcher, she always felt under attack.

The miners had, at that point, downed tools for a whole year, the coffers were empty and the miners were at loggerheads and many of them bankrupt. It was a serious defeat for the British Labour movement and no one dared strike after that, knowing that the government would not climb down. The power of the unions was shattered. One can see this in a positive or negative light but for Mrs. Thatcher it was a historic achievement as Prime Minister.

Her other great achievement was the victory in the Falklands. Galtieri, Argentine's dictator, had simply sent his troops to seize this group of South American islands and occupy them. There were not enough English troops there to resist. However, Mrs. Thatcher said: "We may no longer be a world power, but you cannot do that to my territory. We shall reconquer the islands." She sent the British navy, which took a while but once they got there it took only a few days to oust the Argentineans. It was, possibly, not worth the effort but Thatcher had proved "You cannot just do anything you like with us."

What she never understood throughout her life was a concept of Europe and how important Europe was for England. She never endorsed a role for England in Europe, she always said 'No'. Another factor was that she did not get on with Helmut Kohl. When she came back from a summit meeting in Paris in 1990, she knew that she no longer had the support from her government. She had a meeting with each member of her cabinet, with a possible exception of one or two, and they all said: "Prime Minister - the time has probably come for you to step down." So that is when the Chief Secretary in Downing Street called Buckingham Palace with the message that the Prime Minister would like to come within the next hour in order to resign. We now have that historic picture of Mrs. Thatcher leaving Downing Street in her official car on her way to the Palace, with tears in her eyes. It is an impressive photograph and is symbolic of her leadership.

Willy's mother Charlotte, widowed Hofler, around 1980 in a
restaurant on a trip

My mother

I have nothing but lovely and happy memories of my mother. Whenever I think about her I smile. We always had a good relationship and liked travelling together. There was, above all, a practical side to this as I was the only member of the family that was still around. I did chide myself sometimes for not doing enough for her.

There was a travel agency in England that offered good value short trips to European capitals. We had visited Prague, Rome and Paris but it was Nice that we liked best. So, as long as my mother could still travel, it was to the South of France that we flew several times.

It was always the same routine: Friday morning my mother went to the hairdresser. After that we drove up into the mountains above Nice and went to a Café with a wonderful view over the bay. That left us another couple of hours before the evening service at the Synagogue that I wanted to attend. So I would say to my mother: "We can either turn right and go to the Matisse Museum or drive down into town to do some shopping at the Galeries Lafayette." My mother smiled and said: "You know where I would like to go, but please don't tell your brother!"

Jo, the academic who was in Australia, could never have understood that we preferred going shopping rather than visiting a museum to admire the work of one of the greatest painters of the 20th century. But that is what we enjoyed.

During the last years of her life my mother was bedridden and dependent on assistance. She did not like that but she never complained. She continued to participate in life and even made new friends. Looking back, that was a great achievement. And she finally accepted that her life was coming to an end.

My mother was a brave woman, a fact that she proved on several occasions. When her husband was sent to a psychiatric clinic, she had to cope with the situation alone. When I think of her life, she was always brave when, for example, contrary to accepted conventions, she lived with a man while she was still married to another one. She also had to cope with the fact that two of her three children died an unnatural death.

Perth

About a fortnight before I officially became a Rabbi, my twin brother in Australia committed suicide. When the news came through, it was a Friday evening, I was with my mother in London. For her it was a huge blow, a dreadful blow. I know that at one point that evening I said to myself: "Nothing worse can ever happen in my life." And nothing worse has ever happened again.

The next evening I flew to Australia for the funeral. My mother was already on nursing care and could not come. Because she was dependent on me, I flew back the day after the funeral.

I have been asked what had been the problem with my brother, why did he commit suicide - it was all due to illness. In my father's family there had been psychiatric problems that resulted in a symptom, an urge to commit suicide. The grandmother suffered from the same problem and so had my father's sister who committed suicide, and finally so did my father. In my generation, it affected my brother. Fortunately neither my sister nor I were affected nor, fortunately, none of my sister's children. So I hope that is the end of that.

What is seldom mentioned is the terrible effect that suicide has on the family. It is very difficult to deal with it. One asks oneself constantly if there was something that one could have done, a question that remains. I do hope that one can ultimately reconcile oneself with one's fate.

On being a Rabbi

I am not a religious official who promotes God. There are those who do because they believe that religion leads to the saving of the soul. I do not have this mental image and it has no place in Judaism, or at least not a predominant one, while it probably does in other religions. It is a debatable subject.

What is wonderful for me as a Rabbi is the ceremony that is part of religious life, especially the religious service that gives me great satisfaction. When I was a Rabbi in England, there was a member of the congregation, a man who was rather difficult. When his mother died I led the funeral ceremony. At the end of the service the man came up to me and thanked me. What had impressed him most deeply, he said, was the dignity of the ceremony. And for me, as the Rabbi, that was and remains the greatest compliment. To honour life has always been of great significance for Jews. It is part of honouring creation as well as honouring God.

The other thing that is important to me as a Rabbi is the contact with people, especially in times of distress. Funerals are more important to me than weddings because one can do more for people at funerals. One can console them and help them cope with a difficult situation. Not so much is demanded at a wedding as people are already enjoying a happy occasion. Basically it is almost irrelevant whether one makes a good or a bad speech. There is a sequence of events like signing a document that one follows. But the personal contribution is minimal.

Sometimes I retain contact with the couple, even after the wedding and sometimes one can be of help. One couple for whom I had performed the marriage ceremony developed some problems. The man phoned me and we had a meal together but he hardly talked about his marriage. At the end of the meal I said to him: "Listen! The basic question is, do you want to stay together or not?" He looked at me in utter astonishment and said that he had not thought about that. So I said to him: "So go home" - well, he would have done that anyway - "and talk to her about it. Do you want to stay together?" So he left and I did not hear any more from him. But a few years later I was invited to the blessing of one of their children. That did give me pleasure and satisfaction.

In my opinion the Rabbi of a congregation should always be available. And that is not really difficult. But

Willy Wolff at a wedding, 1991 in London

some people do differ in regard to this. Some Rabbis insist on having one free day a week. I never wanted that. I am a workhorse and like working.

When I was a Rabbi in London I stayed at home every Thursday but I told the community: "If anyone wants to talk to me, they can phone me at home." Such a call probably took two minutes. When I go to the office the next day and there is a list of all the people that I should call, that is a lot more work. I much prefer to go to the telephone at once and have the necessary discussion. Then that is finished and I have a clearer head the following day. But that is a very personal decision.

I do not like working with e-mails. I do have a mobile in case I am delayed when I am going somewhere. Then I can make a call which is why my mobile stays mostly in my car which is a great advantage. If it were turned on all the time it would be a burden for me. I am sure that if anyone needs to speak urgently to me, they will find me.

Lions in Johannesburg

It is rare among the English Jewish community to advertise for a Rabbi. He is generally found through recommendation. One is told: "This or that congregation needs a Rabbi. If you are interested, do apply for it."

My first obligation was to remain in London to look after my mother. So I started as Assistant Rabbi in one of the largest congregations in London. I really liked it there. It was a wonderful Synagogue with an organ and a choir. I also got on very well with my boss, Rabbi Hugo Gryn, who was born in Czechoslovakia and had survived Auschwitz. We got on very well and I was basically very happy.

Then my mother died and I received an offer from Newcastle in the north of England, where I wound up being Rabbi for four years.

In England they work it out so that members of a congregation finance their own community. If it is a small congregation there is never much money. It happened that a couple of times the congregation was unable to pay. So I spent quite a while looking for another position which meant that I got around a bit which was really interesting.

More than 20 years ago I was in South Africa, in a Community that did not at that time have its own Rabbi. So, every autumn, they engaged a Rabbi, usually from America for the Jewish High Holidays. I don't remember how I heard about this, but I was invited and went there.

I landed in Johannesburg at six o'clock in the morning and at nine o'clock I was in the office. I had to officiate at a burial at 2pm and that evening I led a further funeral service. And so it continued, relentlessly. Word got round: this Rabbi is available in his office every day! So they all came with different problems or just to pop in with a friendly 'hello'. There was a lot of work with no time to look at the country.

After five weeks, on my last day, someone invited me for a drive through the surrounding area. And there, suddenly, in the middle of this scenery, were lions! They were sitting there, absolutely peacefully, but I remained prudently in the car and resisted stroking them. Better not, I told myself. It might be misunderstood.

It was a beautiful time and I would have quite liked to stay in South Africa. But then I said to myself: "Come December and England enjoys the beautiful Christmas period while it's summer here, you'll feel really homesick." So I decided I won't stay.

Windsor

Christmas Eve at the Royal Church in Windsor is first of all a great pleasure and secondly a highlight in my life. It is a very special church service that was introduced by an Anglican vicar at the end of the 19th century. Nine sections of the Bible, all to do with Jesus, are read out and Isaiah's prophecies from the Old Testament or something similar, interspersed with Christmas carols. The congregation members know some of these and sing along, others are sung just by the choir. That is beautiful and a great deal more beautiful than if they were sung just by schoolchildren.

Rabbis are generally not expected to be present at a Christmas service, but I get great pleasure from it. I don't shout about this from the rooftops, certainly not from a Synagogue rooftop. It would certainly create some surprise and I would have to justify myself. But since the Jewish press sends no reporters there, I can do what I like.

I have been going to Windsor with the same friends for the last 50 years or more. This was all due to my then boss of the weekly "Slough Observer". His name was Leslie Tunks and he was a very strict boss. Nevertheless a personal friendship grew between us. One day before Christmas eve, we had just finished the latest edition, Leslie asked me: "And what are you going to do over the holidays?" I replied: "Tomorrow morning early I'm taking a train to Cambridge to queue at the King's College Chapel for the service." You have to know: this is one of the most beautiful churches in England, not only is the building - late gothic - exceptional but the choir is world famous. Every year, on 24 December, there is this Anglican Christmas service. One has to queue up for hours to get in and I was ready to do that.

But then Leslie said: "Why would you want to go to Cambridge? Here in Windsor it is just as beautiful and just as good!" And because Leslie was, for me, a person of authority and I knew that he would ask me later where I had spent Christmas Eve, I did not dare to travel to Cambridge but rather went to Windsor. In later years, Leslie always came with me and afterwards we went to his home, which was close by, where he had organised a cocktail party. And that became a habit. Unfortunately, Leslie died from cancer in 2008. Since then his widow accompanies me to Windsor.

When I am on holiday or if I cannot get to a Synagogue at weekends, I go to a church on Sunday. I just need this relationship with God. I derive something emotional from it even though I don't participate in many of the prayers because they are not compatible with Judaism. After all, we pray to one and the same God. Christians have the additional figure of Christ who plays no part in Judaism. I have always been greatly interested in all forms of religious services and I am very familiar with the Anglican liturgy.

I did, after all, grow up in a Christian environment and the Anglican Church has more influence in English life than the Catholic or Protestant church in Germany. The Church of England is a state church with not only theological influence but with a special role in English culture.

When I went to school in England, our music teacher would play for us mainly records with different kinds of music. One of these records was with the choir of the Russian-Orthodox church in Paris. That was wonderful music, very moving and beautifully sung. When I went to Paris for the first time after the war, I was determined to listen to that choir myself. So, on Saturday evening, I went to the Russian-Orthodox church - wonderful! Anyway, I have always really liked choral music. And the best place to listen to a choir - at any rate in England - is in church where each church has its own choir.

I have a friend, an Anglican vicar, who is responsible for four small congregations. On one of my visits to him he had given a sermon one Sunday at eight o'clock in a small village church. Two elderly ladies had preceded us, both in cassocks. They were the choir and they sang beautifully.

There is a view among some Jews and some Christian denominations, that words alone should be enough. But I don't share that view. Church music and Synagogue music has always been of great significance for me. It is just that music is part of a religious service. Without it, it is unemotional, too unemotional in my opinion.

Rabbi William Wolff reading from the Torah, Schwerin 2014

Organ

According to orthodox Jewish law, it is forbidden to play a musical instrument on the Sabbath. It is classified as work and the regulations regarding which work is allowed and which is not are very strict. But in Liberal Synagogues whose interpretations of the Sabbath laws are not so strict, the organ is played. It had been adopted from the church to make the service more beautiful which led to more music, to a choir and also to an organ.

Meanwhile the organ has disappeared from many liberal Synagogues but originally, when it was first used after 1800, it had become the symbol of liberal Synagogues. In Germany they were called the "Organsynagogues". So an "Organsynagogue" was a liberal Synagogue.

The Commandments

Jews and Christians have the same bible, the same Old Testament, but they put it to completely different use. For Christianity, the later books of the Old Testament, the prophetic ones, are more important because they suggest the coming of Jesus. For Judaism, it is the first five books that are more important because they contain the commandments. According to Jewish teaching - and that is one of the big differences between it and Christianity - the commandments are more important than faith.

It would be an exaggeration to claim that Jews are indifferent to what one believes but faith is not the biggest issue. Faith is just an accepted fact. Without faith there would not be much point to it. But faith alone is not enough. What is most important is observing the commandments, that one should care about the Sabbath, the Jewish dietary laws and the High Holy Days.

There are 613 requirements or laws, but we cannot adhere to all of them. Some 200 of them have to do with temple practice in Jerusalem. The Temple was destroyed in a.d.70 and subsequently Jewish sacrificial services were no longer practised. So that left around 400 commandments.

I have not succeeded in following all commandments but I believe that is true for all human beings. There are many commandments some of which are very strict. According to the commandments, for example, I am not allowed to travel on a Saturday after the morning service. However, I have done that because it was convenient. We are only human, after all.

The first five books of the Old Testament are also called "The five books of Moses" because tradition claims - now refuted by science - that Moses himself wrote them. It is a tradition to recite from the Torah scroll, the text of which has been handwritten on parchment with a quill pen. There is an annual cycle to the reading of the Torah at the service with one section every week. This always starts in autumn and finishes in autumn. On the same day that the final chapter is read, one begins, once again, with chapter one.

When I was Rabbi in the south of England, I took part in talks with an Anglican vicar. It went well first time but on the second occasion there were a lot of questions from the public regarding the books of the prophets and I realised that my answers were not good enough. After the meeting the vicar came up to me and said: "Well, dear Rabbi, you need to know the books of the prophets rather better than you have up to now!" That was a deserved rebuke but the reason is and always has been that what matters in Judaism is that, above all, one reads the first five books. Those I am familiar with and was, even before I took up Rabbinic studies.

Once on a trip with the Conservative party, I was talking to their Press Officer, a Christian believer; I cannot remember how we got on to the subject of the Ten Commandments. He claimed that: "Love your neighbour as yourself" was one of the Ten Commandments. I denied this but he insisted and so we argued back and forth until I said: "There is no point in arguing about that. Let's look it up!" To my amazement he had a Bible with him! But who was right? I was.

While "Love your neighbour as yourself" is a significant verse in Christendom, it comes from the Old Testament, that is the Hebrew Bible. It was Rabbi Akiba, one of the greatest scholars in ancient Jewish history, whom the Romans executed because he had been accused of plotting a revolt, who said: "The commandment 'Love your neighbour as yourself' is the basic principal in Judaism. He did not describe it as the chief commandment because the commandments come from God alone. He said very adroitly: "The fundamental principle in Judaism is: "Love your neighbour as yourself"'. One has to remember that the Christian church emanates from Judaism. Paul was a Jew as, of course, was Jesus.

I personally believe that the Church owes more to Paul than it does to Jesus but that is a subject for Christian theologians rather than for a Rabbi.

Private jet

When I was still working as Assistant Rabbi for the congregation of Rabbi Hugo Gryn, the first thing I did when I got to the Synagogue was to go to the office. One Friday he was sitting there looking somewhat depressed. I asked him what the problem was and he said: "You know, Willy, I've got to write up six talks before Monday." I said: "Hugo, that is absolutely impossible!" I decided again, and that was my own private view, that his secretary was a very nice woman but, in my opinion, not very competent. So I said to him: "You should have someone that is better at organising your engagements!" So he answered, the same he always did when he didn't agree with me: "Don't be silly. That's not an option." I did rather insist that he accepted too many engagements that he travelled all over the place for occasions that were attended by only some twenty or thirty people. "You really must reduce these many engagements that have nothing to do with the congregation." So Hugo looked at me and said: "Yes, but they are the ones that are the most fun." So that was that. And I have to say that he has been, one way or another, an example to me ever since.

When I later became Rabbi in Newcastle I was asked by a couple who were friends of mine, to officiate at their wedding. The actual marriage ceremony was to take place in a London suburb on a Sunday afternoon. However, in Newcastle, the Jewish religious instructions for children and young people, took place on a Sunday morning. I did not actually have to deal with that but I had promised to be there that day and I could not and did not want to cancel it.

However, I had to arrive punctually at this wedding in London. The train journey from Newcastle to London took more than five hours in those days, so that did not work. And flight times were also unsuitable. The only possible way to arrive in time was to charter a plane.

It was an aircraft for three people, the pilot in front and two seats at the back. I was sitting on one seat and a basket full of fresh fruit was on the other. It was wonderful! All I had to do was to get to the airport where a private car drove me across the runway directly to the plane, I got in, sat down and off we flew at a lower altitude than usual so one could more easily recognise the landscape and individual houses. As we were landing I already saw the Synagogue attendant who was waiting for me and I waved to him. And the most wonderful thing was: he waved back.

I have to confess that it had cost a small fortune. But at that time I still had two sources of income, one from the newspaper for which I still wrote regularly and the second from the Jewish community. So I could just about afford it. And years later I still talk about it so it had definitely been worthwhile.

The Chief Rabbi

Among Jews, the local Rabbi is the chief authority in the congregation. In England, however, a number of congregations have come together to appoint a Chief Rabbi who represents all Jewish communities in public life. His religious authority extends only to those congregations that recognise him. I don't know if that involves the majority of congregations, possibly not.

In Jerusalem there are at least two Chief Rabbis. One for the Ashkenazi Jews who come mainly from Eastern Europe and one for the Sephardic Jews who come from Spain, Portugal, North Africa and the Near East. I am afraid I do not know how they get on with each other. I assume they can agree on certain issues, but how it works, I don't know. I believe it must have something to do with individual personalities as to whether they understand each other or not. I regard neither as the ultimate authority. They do not, basically, have anything to do with me and my work and for me it is irrelevant what they say.

There is a lovely story about a shipwrecked man who winds up on a desolate island. As he discovers, there is another stranded human being who turns out to be a religious Jew. So religious, in fact, that he has built two Synagogues on the island. "Why two?" asks the new arrival. So the first one answers: "Well, I needed one Synagogue that I wouldn't dream of attending!"

Ascot

Once, when I was still a freelance journalist, a colleague once said to me: "You know you can get accreditation for the horse races at Royal Ascot. Why don't you go along and see if there is anything interesting to report." That is how I went to Ascot for the first time. It takes place every year in mid-June and it is Royal because the Queen and her family go there and her Majesty's horses participate.

To my great surprise, this outing gave me enormous pleasure. The horses were almost irrelevant but the people were really elegant, everyone was in a good mood and the view of the soft green countryside was so beautiful, that I said to myself: "You must come here regularly, under your own steam!". And that is what I have been doing over more than 40 years. Kathleen, a friend from Newcastle, accompanies me.

Part of going to the races is betting. I do have a strategy - though I cannot claim that it is very successful - I always bet on horses with the best known jockeys. To my mind, the good jockeys can pick the horses they want to ride and certainly they would not choose the worst ones. My friend Kathleen has a different strategy and wins much more often than I do. But I did sometimes return home having won a little, but most of the time it was just fun.

There is a special area in Ascot that is the Royal Enclosure, a section only for the Queen and other wealthy people. Normal mortals might be allowed to join but would need some recommendation. In addition, it is more expensive and there is a strict dress code.

Willy Wolff in appropriate gear for Royal Ascot 2015

Ladies, for example, have to wear hats! The brim has to have a certain width as has the length of the dresses. If the ladies have enough money, they have their own hats made which costs a small fortune. English newspapers publish pages of pictures of all this during the Ascot days.

Men wear top hats and a "morning coat" which, taken literally would imply a coat worn in the morning but that would be quite wrong. It is a knee-length frock coat with curved hems. These are worn in England at ceremonial occasions that happen during the day such as weddings or, in fact, at Ascot. For years I would hire the morning coat with trousers, waistcoat and top hat but one day I said to myself: "If you are going to Ascot every year, you can buy your own outfit."

What is interesting is this: to be in the royal enclosure, you have to have a title. If you are an aristocrat there is no problem, one is Sir, Lord, Viscount or Earl. But if one is just an ordinary human being, "Esquire" will be the official addition to one's name. The badge that I have to pin on at Ascot reads: "William Wolff Esquire". Looking it up in a dictionary it gives the definition as "high-born' which sounds rather ridiculous today "High-born Willy Wolff", but that is an example of English aristocracy. You cannot just be Mister you have to be elevated to Esquire, even if you come from a bourgeois Jewish background.

I did not expect to go to the races every month, but it was great fun once a year. It was just a beautiful, care-free day. Since I stupidly never created my own family, highlights like Ascot in June and Windsor at Christmas are important. For me, they are something to hold onto.

Germany's fate

London is my hometown. I consider myself a Londoner. I know it well and I always know where I am going. Especially when I was working as a journalist in Parliament, I became part of official English life. But the moment that it became clear to me that despite emigration and despite Nazi persecution, my German origin was of significance to me, was on the evening of the tenth of November 1989. That was a Friday and the evening before the Berlin Wall had fallen.

At that time, I was Rabbi in the North of England in charge of the Newcastle community that had a small sister community in Darlington. That particular Friday afternoon I was on my way to Darlington where I had to take the evening service. I heard the broadcast on the car radio that dealt with the fall of the Berlin wall. I don't weep easily but when I heard that, tears came to my eyes. That is how I realised that the fate of Germany could still move me.

At the service I made a direct reference to the fall of the wall and said a prayer of thanks. I just needed to do that. I do not know whether it was of any significance to my English congregation but for me it was very important. In my opinion it was as important an event in European history as was the French Revolution exactly two hundred years earlier.

One always refers to Helmut Kohl as the first Chancellor of a united Germany but in my opinion he was the second Chancellor who united Germany. The first one was Otto von Bismarck who united the many separate

Grand Duchies to create a German nation state. He was certainly one of the most significant statesmen in German history, but, in addition, and for very personal reasons Otto von Bismarck was significant for me. The best piece of history homework I ever produced in London was an essay about Bismarck. I got twenty out of twenty for a faultless piece. So, even now, I am exceedingly grateful to Herr von Bismarck and still think very highly of him.

Wimbledon

At some time in the mid 1990's Wimbledon lost its Rabbi. I knew the congregation from my period of training and later officiated there on a number of occasions. When they offered me the job of Rabbi for the community, I accepted with pleasure. It was a serious and important appointment.

The world-famous tennis courts were less than a kilometre from our community. During the big Wimbledon championships I noticed that the people living locally earned some money by offering parking facilities on their property. So, instead of visitors finding a space for their cars in the large, official parking area - which was expensive and took a long time to get out of in the evening - they were able to park them normally just a few streets away.

I saw this and suggested to my congregation: "We have such a lot of space here and could easily take 20 cars. We could take £10 a day which is competitive. That way we would get £200 a day for a whole week. That adds

Willy Wolff in his kitchen, Henley-on-Thames 2015

up to something!" And that is what we did. But our care-taker did not want to come on a Sunday, his day off, to open the gates. So that is when I went and collected the money. That was great fun and brought in a few thousand pounds.

A number of our community were elderly and I thought it would be a good idea to offer them something of interest. So I initiated a monthly lunch. We always invited some interesting person who would give a talk, someone who lived in the area, a politician, an actress or whoever. The community always thought that everyone that came was a friend of mine. That was not always the case. Some, but not all of them, were acquaintances.

I read in the newspaper, for example, that an English diplomat, who had been a former UK Ambassador in an Arab country, was living in Wimbledon. I found his address in the telephone directory and he accepted immediately. I picked him up and he gave a very interesting talk and people could ask him questions. He was considered pro-Arab and anti-Israel, but that was not the case.

These lunches were always pleasant events. It did not involve great effort but provided, above all, a great deal for the older members of the community. We called it: "Food for Thought".

Then the Community appointed a new chairman, a doctor, a very clever man. But I did not get on well with him. On one occasion, the head of the Reform movement in England said to me: "Listen, the head of your Wimbledon community is worried about your age." I was 75 at the time but I said to myself right then: "Well,

I know a place where they don't worry about that." So I phoned Berlin and told them that I was ready to come to Germany."

Mecklenburg-West Pomerania

A few years earlier I had got to know Peter Fischer from the Central Council for Jews in Germany. He was responsible for the newly founded communities in the new Federal States and he always said: "We need Rabbis here!"

After the reunification the German Federal Government could not envisage a future without Jews, for that would have meant success for Hitler's work of destruction. So the Federal States opted for immigration. In the succeeding 15 years some quarter of a million Jews came to the Federal Republic from former socialist East European countries. A certain number of them moved into the new federal states where they did not find any Jewish life nor any Synagogues, let alone Rabbis. There just were no German Jews left or, at least, very few. When I phoned Dr. Fischer in Berlin, he immediately thought of the position in North-East of Germany, in Mecklenburg-West Pomerania, where I had already helped out a few times. To my great delight, the Community there decided to accept me. I took up the appointment of Chief Rabbi in April 2002.

In Mecklenburg I was responsible for the two large communities of the state capitals of Schwerin and the Hanseatic town of Rostock and for the smaller community in Wismar. All three were immigrant communities

Rabbi Willy Wolff at the entrance to the Synagogue of the
Jewish community in Schwerin 2014

without roots or tradition. They had been established some eight years earlier and the members were almost exclusively from the former Soviet Union. I was the only one who was not from Russia or the Ukraine.

None of the members of the community, though there were one or two exceptions, knew anything about Judaism. Only a very few had been able to observe their religion in the Soviet Union. That seems to me one of the big cultural crimes committed by East-European communism. There was no longer any training for the Rabbinate, the communities were refused money, anyone who confirmed his religious beliefs came under suspicion, was expelled from university or lost his job. In the end there was not much Judaism left. I found it not only astonishing but also frightening that a culture can be destroyed so easily. Before I came to Schwerin, I had not been aware of the success of Soviet communism in eradicating Judaism - eradicating is the only word to describe it.

In 1975, when I was still a journalist, I spent ten days in the Soviet Union with the Chief Rabbi, Immanuel Jakobovits who had been invited to visit the Jewish communities there. At that time there was still some Jewish life there, for example in Leningrad. I have never heard a more beautifully sung service as this one in Leningrad. But when I got there again later, there was nothing left. Nothing. There was still a Rabbi in Moscow who was responsible for the whole of the Soviet Union, for three million Jews. What does one Rabbi do with three million Jews?

Aimée and Jaguar

Shortly after my arrival in Schwerin there was a film on television about the love of two women during the Nazi period in Berlin. I did not concern myself further with this - lesbian love stories are of no great interest to me - while bookshops are and when I went there as usual to get my newspaper, there was a pile of books about the film. I did not intend to buy a copy but I did have a quick look and suddenly saw photos of relatives of mine from Berlin.

It transpired that the woman with the nickname "Jaguar" was a second cousin of mine, Felice Schragenheim. Her sister Irene and my sister Ruth were always playing together as kids. Her father Albert, a dentist, called Ali by the family, was not only my father's cousin; my parents were close to him and his wife and they often went out together. But as we emigrated as early as 1933 the contact was lost. I knew that his wife had been killed in a car accident but it was only from the book that I found out that Ali died from a heart attack in 1935 and that the daughter, Irene, emigrated to London, just as we did. Felice was the only one to remain in Berlin hoping to survive underground. She started a love affair with a non-Jewish woman but was arrested, deported and never came back from Auschwitz.

This story was first published in a book "Aimée and Jaguar" by the Berlin journalist Erica Fischer which led to the highly regarded film by Max Färberböck. The love story of these two women achieved cult status in some circles. I do not know whether it does justice to

Felice. Nor do I believe that her parents were particularly pleased with this story. In the book the family is described as not religious but that is not true. I remember one New Year's day when Uncle Ali visited us. He was wearing a top hat. That was what orthodox Jews wore for the High Holy Days in the Synagogue.

The Synagogue in Berlin that my father and our relatives went to was full of men wearing top hats. Later, not many congregations adhered to this custom. As for example in the big London Synagogue in which I was active. Once on a very hot day, the Chairman asked me if it was all right for the wardens to wear a skull-cap instead of a top hat. I immediately answered: "No," because I found that top hats contributed to the solemnity. That is just my personal opinion not based on religion. The head has to be covered but it does not need to be by a top hat.

While I never wore a top hat in Schwerin, people recognised me by my hat. It was expected of me as a Rabbi to have my head covered and that was no problem for me. But it did take a little while before I realised that I was part of public life in Mecklenburg. When I was walking around Schwerin a lot of people greeted me even if I did not know them at all.

The Neo-Nazis, that is the NPD party, who represented Mecklenburg-West Pomerania in Parliament, did not cause me concern. When there was a state election, the North German radio station asked me for my opinion regarding the possible results. My immediate reaction was: "If the NPD gained 7 percent of the votes, it means that 93% of the population did not vote for them. I am proud of my fellow Mecklenburg citizens," I added, and I still am.

I was of the opinion that this ideology no longer appealed to the majority of the population. Of course in East Germany the reason for its popularity was high unemployment. But I do not see it as a threat. We live in a different era.

I was grateful and even a little proud to be living and working in Germany, a country where the events of the past had become unimaginable. An overwhelming majority of Germans have accepted responsibility for the consequences of that past and that gave me a feeling of security.

Only once in all those years did I experience someone making a scurrilous remark. It was evening and the man appeared to be drunk. To be molested just once in thirteen years was for me acceptable. There is an English saying: "If you cannot stand the heat, get out of the kitchen." I share that view.

The Russian congregation

Jewish life stands on two legs, one being the religious services and celebrations and the other is Jewish domestic life. In my opinion we succeeded in Schwerin and Rostock to create an authentic Synagogue life. But I do not know if people kept Jewish holidays and the Sabbath at home. I got the impression that, with a very few exceptions, they did not. People were not used to it and did not know how to celebrate.

To bring Jewishness back into the lives of these people, is an enormous task. I would not like to say that it is impossible, but it would need more people and much more Rabbinic support. I could not do that on my own especially not for two and a half congregations.

The Schwerin congregation consisted of 900 members of whom some 30 or 40 attended the weekly services with some 200 attending the High Holiday services in autumn. That meant that I had almost never seen 700 of them. It sounds like a paradox, but some members I got to know only when they were dead. If they wanted to be buried according to Jewish tradition I had to officiate and write a funeral speech.

It is difficult to keep a kosher home in Mecklenburg. Where would you get kosher meat? There is not a single Jewish butcher in Mecklenburg. To get the meat from Berlin or Hamburg would cost a small fortune. As a result, no one here keeps a kosher home. One has to be aware of that.

Rabbi Willy Wolff in front of the Ark of the Schwerin
Synagogue, 2014

Russian lessons

The big difference between Schwerin and Rostock is that there were jobs in Rostock but hardly any in Schwerin. That made integration difficult in Schwerin because the unemployed stuck together and learned hardly any German.

When I got to Mecklenburg I had, first of all, to understand that migration today is completely different from the time that my family and I were emigrants. On both occasions, first in Holland and then in England, my mother had to learn the language immediately otherwise we would have starved. In those days there were no self-service stores so one had to speak Dutch or English to get what one wanted. That is no longer necessary today. Many members of the community live in the same area of town, watch Russian television and go shopping in supermarkets. They do not need to speak German to do that.

You cannot oblige people to learn German. If I wanted to communicate with the congregation I had to speak the language that they spoke. So, once a week, I took Russian lessons with Olga Korneeva in Schwerin. That gave me a great deal of pleasure. Even now, while I unfortunately do not speak Russian particularly well, I can make myself understood. I conducted the services partly in Hebrew and partly in the local language which, for the Mecklenburg congregation, was Russian. There are Russian prayer books where the Hebrew text is written in Russian characters. My sermons were translated into Russian and in Schwerin I also delivered them in Russian.

I was occasionally asked to which movement the community in Mecklenburg belonged. I answered: "We don't need to belong to a movement. We are the only Jewish community in Mecklenburg, full stop!" I think we developed our own rites, somewhere between orthodox and liberal. We are not seriously orthodox because the weekly section from the Bible is recited in Russian, which would be totally unimaginable for an orthodox congregation. But, at the same time, we are not genuinely liberal either since the women of the congregation do not have equal status. They are not allowed to read from the Torah nor recite prayers, something I personally regretted. But the most influential members of the community had been against it and, had I insisted, I would only have caused ongoing dispute. And that I certainly did not want. It is one of my few principles that the job of a Rabbi is to avoid a split in the community at all costs. That is very important for me and I believe I did succeed in that in Mecklenburg.

Bowing out

I really like my work. I cannot imagine life without work. During my time in Mecklenburg I shuttled back and forth every two or three weeks taking a train to Hamburg and from there by plane to Heathrow. An hour and a half later I was on English soil. I always really liked being in Schwerin and Rostock but I knew the appointment would come to an end one day so my little house near Henley has remained my home. There is an English saying "Your home is where your heart is." For me it is where my books are. But then, too, most of my closest friends are in England.

I have asked myself if the Mecklenburg-West Pomerania congregation ever regretted taking me on. My most useful contribution to their community was probably that I created and kept up friendly relations with local and national government. The community had language problems and of course it is difficult to cope with German bureaucracy. I am sure that my presence helped to improve relations with public authorities and local government and at the same time I made good friends. And I greatly valued my growing friendship with Dr. Armin Jäger, the long term Interior minister of Mecklenberg and civic leader of Schwerin.

I should have liked to continue working until my 90th birthday and our community leader Valeriy Bunimov was prepared to extend my contract, but then at a board meeting it was decided that I should finish. I do believe, but I am not sure, that it had to do with the fact that this was a Russian congregation and I was not Russian. Then I actually understood that what they really wanted

Willy Wolff in the Hansa quarter of Berlin, 2014

was someone like themselves. I was not hurt nor was I surprised because I was very aware of the fact that I am different from them.

The custom in England is that when a vicar retires he must leave the congregation. That is not a legal requirement but rather a tradition. He is not allowed to stay so as not to compete with his successor. It would be unpleasant for everyone if, after the Sunday service, the congregation were to flock to the erstwhile vicar rather than to the new one. The old one should leave the field open to the new one. I always regarded that as a good rule.

Honorary citizen

A year before the end of my contract with the Jewish community of Mecklenburg, the members of the town council of Schwerin decided to grant me honorary citizenship. This touched me greatly. I was probably the first Jew but certainly the first Chief Rabbi of Mecklenburg who was honoured in this way. But this honour also involved an obligation on my part. I thought that Schwerin should be my last resting place.

My friends and relatives in England were not particularly delighted by this idea. My nephews in America and in Israel said that, when I had passed away, they wanted to visit my grave and it would be much more difficult to get to Schwerin than to London. Schwerin just was not on one of the public highways of this world.

I had already reserved a grave in London, in the same

cemetery that my mother has a grave. If I had children, I would leave the decision to them but since I do not, I have to make the legal provision myself. My ultimate decision was that I should be buried where I died. If I die in England, then it should be London and if in Germany, then Schwerin. It seems quite crazy to me to fly a corpse this way or that.

Ultimately it is unimportant in which cemetery I will be buried. According to Jewish law all tombstones should be uniform. We should be in similar, simple coffins made of wood without decoration. There should not even be handles. With that, Judaism stresses that all human beings are equal, especially before God. Whatever we may have achieved in life or not, our human souls are basically the same. That appears to me as a beautiful idea: something remains that cannot be judged by worldly success.

The end

I have never had a 'leitmotiv', a guiding principle, for my life. I really like being on this earth and this deep feeling comes from my innermost being. I also never think about what happens when my life ends. Jewish teaching tells us that the soul survives in a different dimension that it calls "Olam Haba" the "next world". Whether I believe in that or not does not cause me worries. I am prepared to be surprised. If nothing happens I shall just have been so many years on this planet and that is that.

However, I am fairly sure that there is another existence in a different dimension that is beyond our comprehension. The great scholar Moses Ben Maimon, known as Maimonides - in my opinion the greatest Jewish scholar of the last 2000 years - wrote something very beautiful: "Just as a fish cannot imagine what life is like on land as he lives in water, so we human beings cannot imagine what happens in the world to come."

What is frequently mentioned, also by Jewish people, is that there we shall meet again those that we loved here on Earth. I would dearly like to see again those people that had meant something to me, for example my mother. I would know what to ask her right away, that is: "Mother, where are we driving to? What can we have a look at?" However, my problem is: if I meet those that I loved here on earth, what about those that I didn't love? There are people that I have seen enough of here on earth. Would I meet them too?

Unfortunately, there is no answer to that until one gets there. Apparently in the next world there are no mobiles. When I do find out one of these days - sooner rather than later - I shall not be able to phone anyone to tell them: "That's what it looks like here". I do regret that since my first job was working as a reporter.

Maybe Archangel Gabriel, or whoever looks after erstwhile Rabbis in the next world, will allow me to send a brief account down to earth of life up there. Until that moment, however, I shall enjoy every day of life here on earth.

Willy Wolff at his home, Henley-on-Thames, 2014

Postscript by Britta Wauer

I met Willy Wolff for the first time in May 2008 during the preparation for my film "In Heaven, Underground," which was about the Weissensee Jewish cemetery in Berlin. What I was looking for at that time was a kind of narrator for the film, a Rabbi who could convey not only the differences between Jewish and Christian mourning rituals but also the concept of the afterlife in Judaism. Anna Fischer from the Centrum Judaicum thought of consulting Willy Wolff, born in Berlin, who was the State Rabbi of Mecklenburg-West Pomerania in North-East of Germany. The first time I met Willy Wolff he was in Berlin for a Rabbinical conference. He was sitting in a coffee-house next to the Synagogue in the Oranienburger Street and immediately agreed to participate.

I had no idea that he would contribute to the making of the film, in addition to his Rabbinic knowledge, both acting talent and a great sense of humour. That had been a stroke of luck for the film about the Weissensee cemetery. Although he was only a secondary figure, he succeeded in making something that had seemed impossible: he was witty, intelligent and charming when he was talking about death, mourning and the concept of the Hereafter. When the film premiered at the 2011 Berlin Film Festival, the Rabbi was the star of the show.

It did not matter where on earth "In Heaven, Underground" was shown - whether at festivals in Beijing, Toronto, New York or Johannesburg, cinema audiences would always shake with laughter at William Wolff's words. "He could convert me to religion!," a member of a London audience called out. Someone in Jerusalem said what was special about Willy Wolff's unusual worldly wisdom was "a rare mixture of East European Jewish wit and British humour." Whenever I spoke in public I was asked to talk about this gentleman. The more information I gave about Willy Wolff, the more obvious it became that I should make a film about him.

Four years later "Rabbi Wolff" is completed. It is a 90 minute documentary about an unusual man who, while bestowing a wonderful smile on everyone has had to deal with many blows of fate himself. Apart from his biography that is characterised by flight and emigration, it is also closely connected with post-war European politics. At the same time Willy Wolff is a deeply religious person and a scholar who reflects on life, good fortune and contentment.

It took a little while before I grasped how exceptionally privileged we, the film team, were: not only did we get to know many of his close friends and relatives - all of them impressive people - but we also moved between his different areas of activity. We accompanied him to the Ascot horse races and also to his orthodox relatives in Jerusalem. We observed him at a religious service with a congregation in London and at a Russian lesson in Schwerin. We went together with him to the Fasting Clinic in Bad Pyrmont and to the church in Windsor Castle for the Christmas carols.

We went to the Dead Sea, to the Conference of Chief Rabbis and to the House of Commons. We continued to find new aspects of Willy Wolff and to get to know more and more about his life.

Anyone who has had the great pleasure of knowing Rabbi Wolff personally, would recognise this sentence: "I don't know if I've told you this before….." We spent more than a hundred hours recording conversations with Willy Wolff of which, however, we could only use a fraction in the film. But I thought it a pity to consider the rest as "waste."

I had a thick file of transcribed interviews with Willy Wolff and could not imagine that no one would be interested in the meetings with and the views of the Rabbi. I am most grateful to the publisher, Dr. Nora Pester, for agreeing immediately to publish Willy Wolff's memoir to coincide with the completion of the documentary. However, I have to confess that it contains only a small part of the recorded material but I do hope that we have made a good choice of William Wolff's entertaining, thoughtful and inspiring stories.

Britta Wauer, Berlin, 13 March 2016

Biographical dates

1927   13th February birth of Wilhelm and his twin brother Joachim in Berlin, the family live at the Holsteiner Ufer in the Hansa quarter.

1933   from April: attends the Adass Yisrael Community School in Siegmunds Hof 11
27 September: family emigrates to Amsterdam the children are first put into a children's home in Hilversum

1934   June: father Alfred Wolff returns after several months in Ludwig Binswanger's psychiatric clinic in Switzerland
the family lives in Amsterdam-Zuid, the twins attend the public school and attend the Synagogue in the Lekstraat.

1939   January: Father Alfred Wolff buys a house in the Hendon district of London
28 August: mother Charlotte Wolff arrives in London with the twins

1940   from January: attends Hendon County School, Barnet
February: Bar Mitzvah at the Hendon United Synagogue

1941   the parents' marriage breaks down, in a rest home, mother gets to know a new man, Bernard Hofler and they move in together.

1943   July: end of school with General School Certificate. Willy receives a half stipend for the Lycée Français in London and starts a bilingual course in office work.

1944   starts work at the Reuter press agency in High Barnet in charge of, inter alia, the radio reports from the supreme command of the Wehrmacht.

1946   November: Father Alfred Wolff dies

1947	studies at the London School of Economics (LSE) International Relations and Economics, becomes seriously ill and unable to work for several years.
1954	starts as reporter with the weekly paper "Slough Observer"
1956	becomes parliamentary correspondent of the House of Commons for the "Yorkshire Post" and the "Liverpool Daily Post".
1962	starts his work with the biggest English daily paper "Daily Mirror"
	moves into his house "Little Paddock" near Henley-on-Thames
1964	23 December: sister Ruth is killed in a car accident
1968	at the request of the Editor of the Daily Mirror he changes from home affairs to foreign affairs resulting in a trip with the Foreign Secretary Stewart and again setting foot on German soil for the first time since his emigration
1970	till 1974: a number of times guest at the WDR programme: "International Morning Session" Chair: Werner Höfer
1971	with a woman friend opened a vegetarian restaurant "The Whole Meal" in Upper Street in the London quarter of Islington alongside his work as a journalist
1975	becomes Europe correspondent for the "Daily Mirror"
1977	independent journalist writing mainly for the London "Evening News"
1979	starts rabbinic studies at the Leo Baeck College in London while working as political correspondent for the Scottish Glasgow paper "Sunday Mail"
1984	14 days before receiving the Smicha (ordination

	for the Rabbinate) his twin brother Joachim commits suicide in Perth, Australia.
	becomes Assistant Rabbi under Hugo Gryn at the West London Synagogue.
1985	4 October: mother Charlotte Hofler dies in London
1986	becomes Rabbi of the Newcastle-upon-Tyne community
1990	to Milton Keynes as their first Rabbi
1993	takes over at the Jewish community in Brighton
1997	becomes Rabbi at the Wimbledon & District Synagogue
2001	November: was finalist from among 250 preachers of all denominations at the competition for "The Times Preacher of the Year"
2002	23rd April: becomes State Rabbi of Mecklenburg-West Pomerania and is in charge of the Jewish congregations in Schwerin, Rostock and Wismar
2005	election for the Deputy Chairman of Germany's Conference of Rabbis
2006	receives the honorary doctorate from the Department of Theology of the Ernst-Moritz-Arndt University Greifswald and the Siemerling Social Prize
2007	receives the Order of Merit of the Federal Republic of Germany First Class and the Israel-Jacobson Prize
2014	27 January, becomes Honorary Citizen of the town of Schwerin
2015	31 March: his contract with Mecklenburg-West Pomerania ends, he retains the title "State Rabbi" and continues to fulfil duties assigned to him.

Willy Wolff in Berlin, 2015

Acknowledgments from Britta Wauer

Many people were involved in the creation of the film about Rabbi William Wolff.

Since the book is based on interviews made during the filming in Germany, Great Britain, Israel and the Netherlands, I should like, first of all, to thank my film team, especially Karsten Aurich, Berthold Baule, Felix Heibges and Kaspar Köpke.

I was supported in my research by many friends and Willy Wolff's relatives and I want to thank them all most warmly as well as the following contributors: Kathleen Egleton, Anna Fischer, Eva and Dr. Peter Fischer, Elisheva Friedman, Leo Hepner, Z'l and Regina Hepner-Neupert, Brian Hillman,Z'l, Elsa and Bernadette Hillman, Stefanie Horn, Dr. Armin and Gaby Jäger, Olga Korneeva, Manuela and Udo Koska, Kryss Katsiavriades, Patricia Lassalle, James Leek, Carolyn Naumann, Karla Pilpel, Gabi Ruppin and Brian Shand, Dr Hermann Simon, Helen Spiro, Sarah Thompson, Judith Tunks, Abe Wagschal, Ruth Weinberger, Gabriele Williams and Rabbi Alexandra Wright.

I want to give special thanks to the support I received from the Jewish Community of Mecklenburg-West Pomerania above all from Valeriy Bunimov and Juri Rosov.

I want to thank my family for their support and understanding; and to thank my friends Asita Behzadi, Claudia Bissinger, Janina Dahse, Tamara Dietl, Antonie Kerwien, Amélie Losier and Susanne Utzt for their support and encouragement.

Many thanks also to Becky Fullerton, Neele Kilanowski, Laura Köpke, Almut Pape, Mia Sellmann and Jana Westmann who helped with the transcript of the interviews.

Many thanks for Uli Holz for the cover illustration and other beautiful photos of Willy Wolff. I thank both, Sarah Pohl for the editing and Michaela Weber for the design of the Original German edition. Many thanks also to Dr. Nora Pester for her great cooperation.

My special thanks go to Rabbi William Wolff who always received us warmly and who shared so much of his time and life experiences with us.

Picture credits:

Elsa Hillman, London (p.71); Uli Holz, Berlin (p.36, 59, 78, 86, 90, 93, 99, 103, 108, 115) Kryss Katsiavriades, London (p. 55) Abe Wagschal, Cincinnati (p.8, 11, 15, 17, 20, 23, 26, 31, 33, 42); Willy Wolff, Henley-on-Thames (p. 10, 46, 48, 66)

Legal disclaimer: Despite careful research we were not able to locate all rights holders. If you are the creator of any of the photos or know that person, please contact the publisher.

William Wolff

Born 1927 to a Jewish family in Berlin, he lived in England from the age of 12. Willy Wolff worked as a journalist before he became a Rabbi after he turned 50. As a political correspondent of a number of English daily papers he covered world politics closely for three decades. He travelled to China and the Soviet Union with the British Foreign Secretary and met European heads of government. He gave up this life in order to satisfy his wish to become a Rabbi. From 2003, Willy Wolff, in his capacity as Sate Rabbi of Mecklenburg-West Pomerania, looked after the Jewish communities in Schwerin, Rostock and Wismar whose membership consists almost exclusively of immigrants from the former Soviet Union. His own home, however, is near London.

Britta Wauer

 © Kaspar Köpke.

Born 1974 in Berlin is regarded as one of the most prestigious film directors of her generation. She has directed and produced documentaries focusing mainly on contemporary history, current affairs and biographies. In 2005 she founded the independent production company Britzka Film. There, she released her 2011 feature documentary "In Heaven, Underground", covering the story of the Weissensee Jewish Cemetery of Berlin, which received among others the Audience Award at the Berlin International Film Festival 2011. Britta Wauer gives lectures at home and abroad and has led workshops on documentary filming in Beijing, Cape Town, Vienna and Washington DC.

CPSIA information can be obtained
at www.ICGtesting.com
Printed in the USA
BVOW08s0957231216
471731BV00001B/57/P